At Sylvan, we believe reading is one of life's most important and enriching abilities, and we're glad you've chosen our resources to help your child build this critically important skill. We know that the time you spend with your children reinforcing the lessons learned in school will contribute to their love of reading. This love of reading will translate into academic achievement. Successful readers are ready for the world around them, ready to do research, ready to experience the world of literature, and prepared to make the connections necessary to achieve in school and in life.

We use a research-based, step-by-step process in teaching reading at Sylvan that includes thought-provoking reading selections and activities. As students increase their success as readers, they become more confident. With increasing confidence, students build even more success. Our Sylvan Page Per Day books are designed to help you to help your child build the skills and confidence that will contribute to your child's success in school.

Included with your purchase of this Page Per Day book is a coupon for a discount at a participating Sylvan center. We hope you will use this coupon to further your child's academic journey. To learn more about Sylvan and our innovative in-center programs, call 1-800-EDUCATE or visit www.SylvanLearning.com.

We look forward to partnering with you to support the development of a confident, well-prepared, independent learner.

The Sylvan Team

Tips for Reading Success

Read with your child every day. This will help your child build a love of reading and be a great opportunity to spend quality time together. It is important to read aloud to your child—even if he or she can already read independently. This activity reinforces a love of reading and can improve your child's vocabulary.

Read with expression. Instill the spirit of the story into your reading. This will also model appropriate reading for your child.

Practice patience. When your child is learning to sound out words and read on his or her own, be patient. If your child gets stuck, offer a gentle reminder and let the reading continue.

Play sound and word games. Tongue twisters and games that focus on where sounds occur in words, e.g., What's the first sound in *cat*?, help increase your child's ability to differentiate and recognize sounds.

Ask your child questions about the story. Talk about what might happen in the story. Stop now and then to ask your child questions and encourage active participation. After reading, discuss the story, asking "wh" questions (*who, what, why, when, where*).

Connect stories to your child's experiences. A child can better enjoy and engage in a story when it relates to fun memories. It also can help you discuss the story and compare it to those experiences.

Go to the library. Help your child value the incredible world of books. Let your child pick out books that he or she finds appealing.

Kindergarten Page Per Day: Reading Skills

Copyright © 2012 by Sylvan Learning, Inc.

Published in the United States by Random House, Inc., New York, and in Canada by Random House of Canada Limited, Toronto.

www.tutoring.sylvanlearning.com

Producer & Editorial Direction: The Linguistic Edge
Writer: Erin Lassiter
Cover and Interior Illustrations: Duendes del Sur
Layout and Art Direction: SunDried Penguin

First Edition

ISBN: 978-0-307-94457-3
ISSN: 2161-9816

This book is available at special discounts for bulk purchases for sales promotions or premiums. For more information, write to Special Markets/Premium Sales, 1745 Broadway, MD 6-2, New York, New York 10019 or e-mail specialmarkets@randomhouse.com.

PRINTED IN THE USA

10 9 8 7 6 5 4 3

What's My Sound?

CIRCLE the pictures that start with the **m** sound. COLOR all the pictures for fun.

Mm

What's My Sound?

DRAW lines from the "Ss" to pictures that start with the **s** sound. COLOR all the pictures for fun.

Ss

Ff

Hide and Seek

LOOK at the farm. CIRCLE at least six things
that start with the **f** sound.

What's My Sound?

CIRCLE the pictures that start with the l sound. COLOR all the pictures for fun.

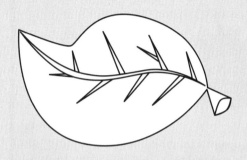

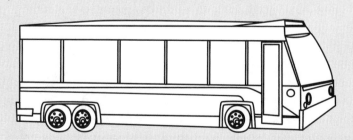

Rr

What's My Sound?

DRAW lines from the "Rr" to pictures that start with the **r** sound. COLOR all the pictures for fun.

Rr

Draw It

LOOK at the train. DRAW your own pictures that start with the **t** sound on the blank train cars.

T t

Hide and Seek

Look at the park. CIRCLE at least 10 things and activities in the park that start with the **p** sound.

Pp

What's My Sound?

DRAW lines from the "Nn" to pictures that start with the **n** sound. COLOR all the pictures for fun.

Nn

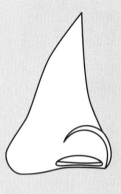

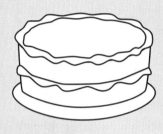

Nn

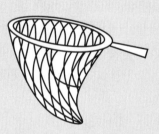

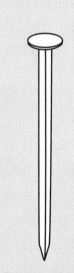

Bb

Draw It

LOOK at the big bag. DRAW your own pictures of things that start with the **b** sound inside the big bag.

What's My Sound?

DRAW lines from the "Cc" to pictures that start with the **c** sound. COLOR all the pictures for fun.

Cc

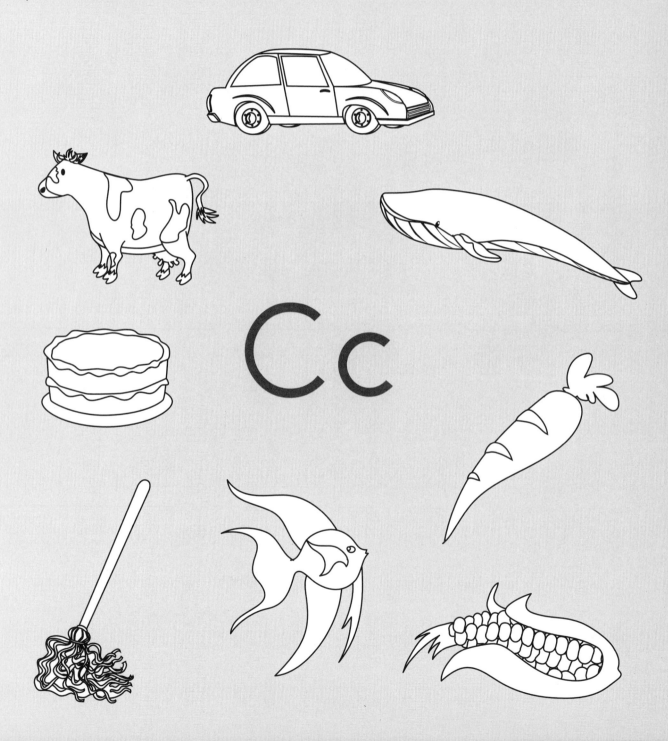

Cc

Hide and Seek

LOOK at the house. CIRCLE at least six things and activities in the house that start with the **h** sound.

What's My Sound?

CIRCLE the pictures that start with the **g** sound. COLOR all the pictures for fun.

Gg

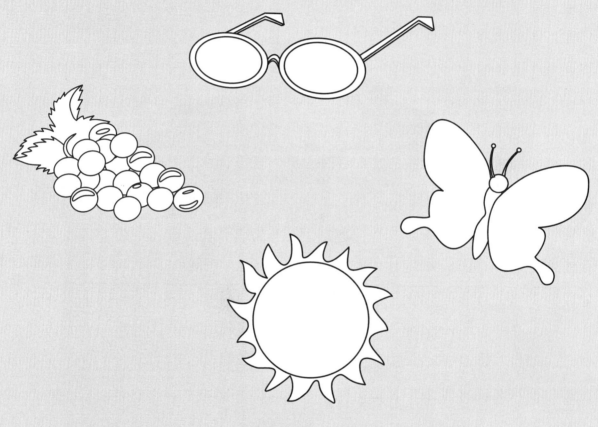

What's My Sound?

DRAW lines from the "Ww" to pictures that start with the **w** sound. COLOR all the pictures for fun.

What's My Sound?

CIRCLE the pictures that start with the **v** sound. COLOR all the pictures for fun.

Dd

What's My Sound?

CIRCLE the pictures that start with the **d** sound. COLOR all the pictures for fun.

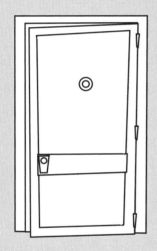

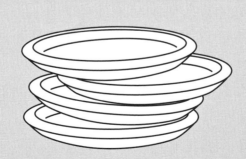

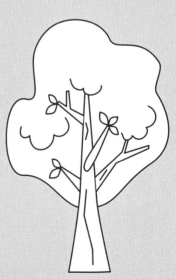

What's My Sound?

DRAW lines from the "Jj" to pictures that start with the **j** sound. COLOR all the pictures for fun.

Jj

Jj

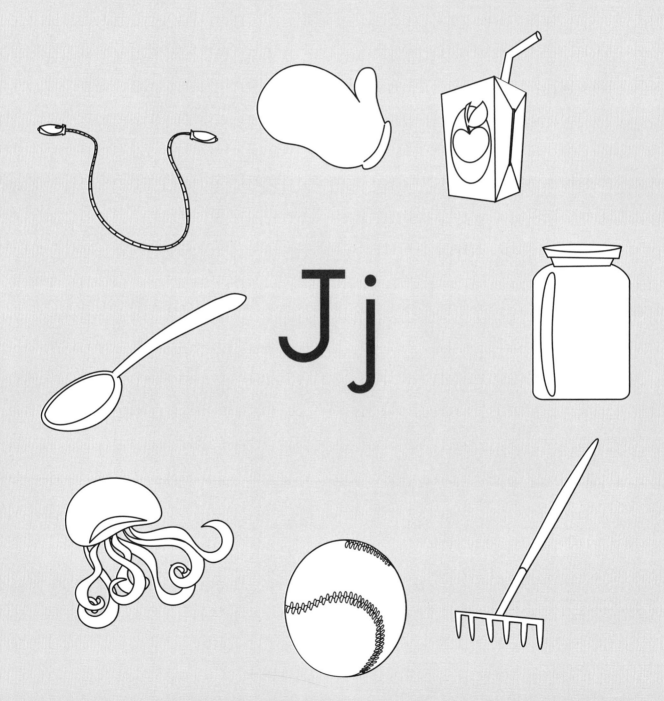

Kk

What's My Sound?

DRAW lines from the "Kk" to pictures that start with the **k** sound. COLOR all the pictures for fun.

Kk

Draw It

X x

LOOK at the box. In the box, DRAW your own pictures of things that have the **x** sound in them.

NOTE: Words that contain the sound but not the letter, such as **socks**, are okay.

What's My Sound?

CIRCLE the pictures that start with the y
sound. COLOR all the pictures for fun.

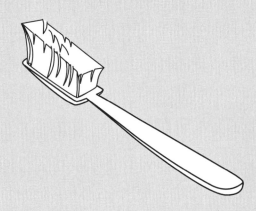

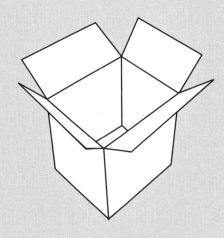

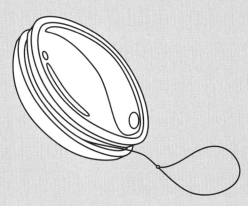

What's My Sound?

DRAW lines from the "Zz" to pictures that start with the **z** sound. COLOR all the pictures for fun.

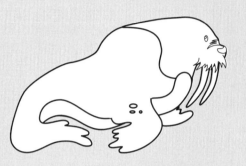

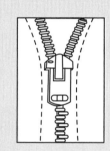

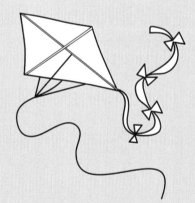

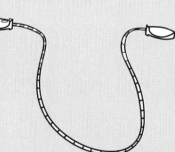

What's My Sound?

DRAW lines from the "qu" to pictures that start with the **qu** sound. COLOR all the pictures for fun.

qu

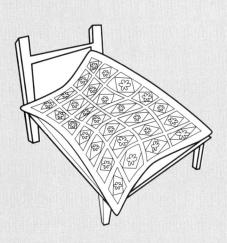

qu

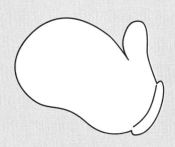

What's My Sound?

DRAW lines from the "ck" to pictures that end with the **ck** sound. COLOR all the pictures for fun.

ck

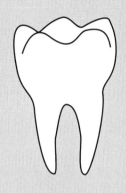

ck

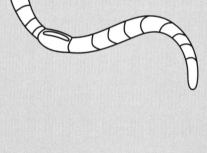

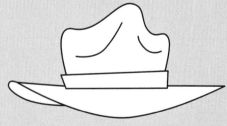

Match Up

LOOK at the pictures. DRAW a line between the pictures that **begin** with the same sound.

Beginning Sounds

Match Up

LOOK at the pictures. DRAW a line between the pictures that **begin** with the same sound.

Circle It

LOOK at the letter. CIRCLE the picture in the row that **begins** with the letter sound.

Hh

Nn

Rr

Ww

Starting Line

LOOK at the picture. WRITE the lowercase letter that makes the sound at the **beginning** of the word.

1

2

3

4

5

6

Match Up

LOOK at the pictures. DRAW a line between the pictures that **end** with the same sound.

Match Up

LOOK at the pictures. DRAW a line between the pictures that **end** with the same sound.

Circle It

LOOK at the letter. CIRCLE the picture in the row that **ends** with the letter sound.

Tt

Ww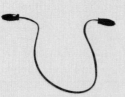

Gg

Dd

Finish Line

LOOK at the picture. WRITE the lowercase letter that makes the sound at the **end** of the word.

_____

- - - - - - - - - - - - - - - - - - -

_____

1   2   3

_____

- - - - - - - - - - - - - - - - - - -

_____

4   5   6

What's My Sound?

DRAW lines from the "a" to pictures with the short **a** sound.
COLOR all the pictures for fun.

a

What Am I?

MATCH the pictures to the words.

hat

pan

rat

bag

cat

What's My Sound?

DRAW lines from the "e" to pictures with the short **e** sound.
COLOR all the pictures for fun.

What Am I?

MATCH the pictures to the words.

web

hen

ten

10

net

bed

What's My Sound?

DRAW lines from the "i" to pictures with the short i sound.
COLOR all the pictures for fun.

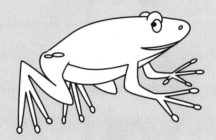

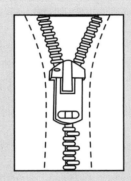

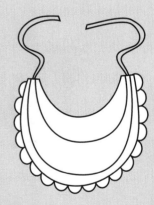

Short Vowel

What Am I?

MATCH the pictures to the words.

kick

bib

pig

sit

kid

What's My Sound?

DRAW lines from the "o" to pictures with the short **o** sound.
COLOR all the pictures for fun.

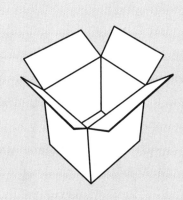

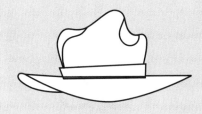

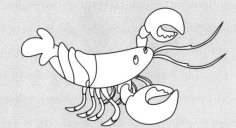

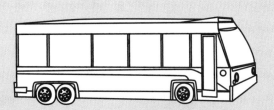

What Am I?

MATCH the pictures to the words.

rod

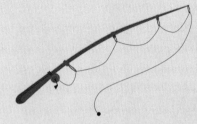

pot

top

mop

box

What's My Sound?

DRAW lines from the "u" to pictures with the short **u** sound.
COLOR all the pictures for fun.

What Am I?

MATCH the pictures to the words.

cup

tub

mud

bug

rug

Who Is It?

The people and the animals in a story are the **characters**.

Animals    # People

CIRCLE the pictures that can be characters in a story.

Who Is It?

READ the story out loud.

The Mud

The pig is in the mud. The dog is in the mud. The rat is in the mud. The hen is in the mud. The mud is brown. The mud is wet. It is fun.

CIRCLE the characters in the story.

Who Is It?

READ the story out loud.

The Mat

The duck ran to the man. The cat ran to the man. The duck sat on the mat. The cat sat on the mat. The man fed the duck and the cat on the mat.

CIRCLE the characters in the story.

Who Is It?

READ the story out loud.

> ### The Rat
>
> A kid sat on a big rock. A dog sat on the rock. A cat sat on the rock. The kid said, "I see a rat." The cat ran. The dog ran. The kid ran.

DRAW the characters in the story.

Where Is It?

The place and time in a story create the **setting**.

Place

Time

CIRCLE the pictures that can be the setting for a story.

Where Is It?

READ the story out loud.

The Cat

I look for the cat. I look on the bed. The cat is not on the bed. I look on the rug. The cat is not on the rug. I look in a big box. I see the cat. It is in the big box.

CIRCLE the setting for the story.

Where Is It?

READ the story out loud.

The Run

He can run. She can run. I can run. You can run. We run to the rock. We run to the log. It is hot. We run in the sun.

CIRCLE the setting for the story.

Story Setting

Where Is It?

READ the story out loud.

The Van

The sun is up. Dad is in the van. I get in the van. We look at the map. We go up a hill. We go down a hill. We go and go in the van.

DRAW the setting of the story.

What's the Order?

READ the story out loud.

Jam and Ham

I have a pot. I put ham in the pot. I put jam in the pot. I mix the ham and jam. Yum!

WRITE 1, 2, and 3 to show the beginning, middle, and end of the story.

_____ _____ _____

What's the Order?

A story has a beginning, a middle, and an end.

LOOK at the pictures. WRITE 1, 2, and 3 to show the correct order.

_____ _____ _____

_____ _____ _____

What's the Order?

READ the story out loud. DRAW the beginning, middle, and end of the story.

The Dog

I put the dog in the tub. I rub the dog. I put the dog in the sun.

1	2	3

What's the Order?

READ the story out loud. DRAW the beginning, middle, and end of the story.

The Cat Nap

I sit on the bed. I pat the cat.

I take a nap with the cat.

1	2	3

What's the Solution?

Most stories have a problem and a solution.

For example:

| Problem | Solution |

LOOK at the problem. DRAW the solution.

| Problem | Solution |

What's the Solution?

LOOK at the problem.

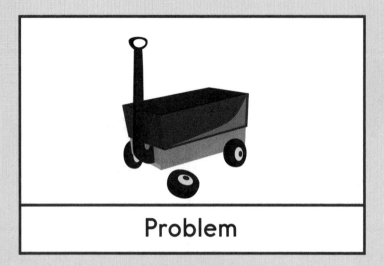

Problem

CIRCLE the correct solution to the problem.

Solution?   Solution?

Page 3

mouse, moon, mitten, map, monkey

Page 4

sun, snail, stop, spoon, star

Page 5

fish, fence, frog, flies, flowers, farmer, face, fruit, flag, fan

Page 6

leaf, lightbulb, ladybug, ladder

Page 7

rainbow, rocket, robot, ring, rake

Page 8

Suggestions: tree, top, teeth, toothbrush, turkey, TV, table, toys, teacher, tea, tie, telephone

Page 9

police, play, path, picnic, pizza, piece of pizza, pie, purse, parrot, paint, painter, painting, person, puppy, post, picnic basket

Page 10

nose, net, nail, nine, nest

Page 11

Suggestions: bat, bug, boy, bread, butter, bottle, bone, bowl, button, bow, balloon, banana, belt

Page 12

car, carrot, corn, cake, cow

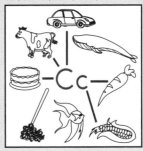

Page 13

ham, horse, hat, hang, hanger, hammer, heart, hair, hat stand, hands

Page 14

glasses, girl, goat, grapes

Page 15

whale, wagon, walrus, worm, window

Answers

Page 16

volcano, violin, van, vegetables

Page 17

door, dress, dishes, doll

Page 18

juice box, jar, jellyfish, jump rope

Page 19

kitten, kangaroo, kick, key

Page 20

Suggestions (can contain letter or sound): ox, taxi, fox, box, ax, six, rocks, socks, trucks, ducks, names with the **x** sound like Max or Rex

Page 21

yarn, yo-yo

Page 22

zebra, zipper, zoo

Page 23

quilt, question mark, queen

Page 24

sock, backpack, truck, duck

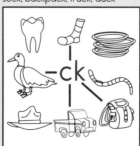

Page 25

Page 26

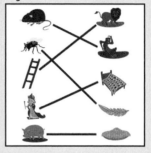

Page 27

Hh
Nn
Rr
Ww

Page 28

1. m, 2. c (or k), 3. b, 4. d, 5. s, 6. l

Page 29

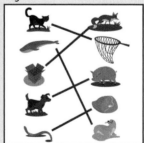

Page 30

Page 31

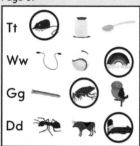

Tt
Ww
Gg
Dd

Page 32

1. n, 2. t, 3. l
4. m, 5. s, 6. g

Page 33

fan, map, rat, ham, bat

Page 34

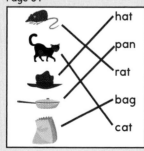

hat
pan
rat
bag
cat

Page 35

nest, net, egg, dress, bed

Page 36

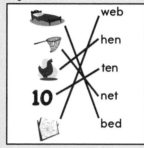

web
hen
ten
net
bed

Page 37

pig, zipper, fish, six, bib

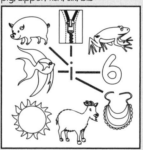

Page 38

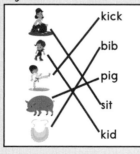

kick
bib
pig
sit
kid

Page 39

dog, lobster, mop, socks, box

Page 40

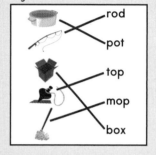

rod
pot
top
mop
box

Page 41

plug, drum, bus, duck, thumb

Page 42

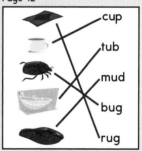

cup
tub
mud
bug
rug

Answers

Page 43
queen, cow, doctor, lion

Page 44
pig, dog, rat, hen

Page 45
man, cat, duck

Page 46
Pictures of a kid, a dog, a cat, and a rat

Page 47
house, barn, night

Page 48

Page 49

Page 50
Picture of a van on a road

Page 51

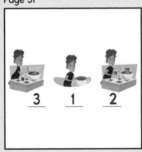

3   1   2

Page 52

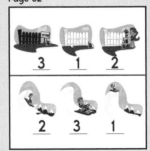

3   1   2

2   3   1

Page 53
Pictures should match the story sequence.

Page 54
Pictures should match the story sequence.

Page 55
Picture should show a solution to the problem.

Page 56

Problem

Solution?   Solution?

With just a **PAGE PER DAY**, your child gets extra practice ... the easy way! Get sample pages for free!

Whether the goal is to get a jumpstart on new material or to brush up on past lessons, setting aside a small amount of time each day to complete one Sylvan workbook page will help your child review and improve skills, grow self-confidence, and develop a love of learning.

Visit **SylvanPagePerDay.com** to get free workbook printables in the grade of your choice!

 CUT ALONG THE DOTTED LINE

Sylvan Learning.

Check out Sylvan's complete line of offerings!

SINGLE-SUBJECT WORKBOOKS

☑ Pre-K–5th grade

☑ Focus on individual skills and subjects

☑ Fun activities and exercises

3-IN-1 SUPER WORKBOOKS

☑ Pre-K–5th grade

☑ Three Sylvan single-subject workbooks in one package

☑ Perfect practice for the student who needs to focus on a range of topics

A $39 value for just $18.99!

FUN ON THE RUN ACTIVITY BOOKS

☑ Kindergarten–2nd grade

☑ Just $3.99/$4.75 Can.

☑ Colorful games and activities for on-the-go learning

FLASHCARD SETS

☑ Spelling for Kindergarten–2nd grade

☑ Vocabulary for 3rd–5th grade

☑ Includes 230 words to help students reinforce skills

PAGE PER DAY WORKBOOKS

☑ Pre-K–1st grade

☑ Perforated pages—perfect for your child to do just one workbook page each day

☑ Extra practice the easy way!

Try FREE pages today at SylvanPagePerDay.com

839

Sylvan Learning